Well, That's Just Ducky!
A Dog Is Man's Best Therapist

Anthony Giffen & Ducky

Copyright © 2013 Anthony Giffen

ISBN-10: 0615879845
ISBN-13: 978-0615879840 (Anthony Giffen)

DEDICATION

For Foley.

Anthony Giffen & Ducky

CONTENTS

ACKNOWLEDGMENTS

Me: Ducky, we have people to thank.

Ducky: For what?

Me: The book wouldn't have been possible without the encouragement and support of so many people.

Ducky: Like the Mama.

Me: Yup. You might have never entered my life if not for her. And she was completely supportive as I opened up to the world on tumblr and wrote about how I was managing the separation and divorce. Not everyone would have done that.

Ducky: Love the Mama.

Me: Me too.

Ducky: And the people who kept telling you what was wrong with the book while you wrote it.

Me: Only my inner monologue was telling me things were wrong, Ducky. But I think you mean Alexa and Wendy.

Ducky: Yeah. The smart people.

Me: Very smart people. They were the right people to trust with our early drafts and they gave great input and encouragement. I don't think we ever would have gotten past the "Maybe I'll make the posts into a book one day" stage without them.

Ducky: Lazy.

Me: On occasion. But this was about confidence. They made me believe it was possible.

Ducky: Other people did too. Like the people who trespass here all the time.

Me: If you mean our friends, yes. Andy and Jenn were very important to me when I was taking those first few tentative steps towards getting healthy. Jami, Maggi, Nicole, and Sara all saw me at my lowest and still found me to have value.

Ducky: And went on that vacation with you that's in the book.

Me: Yup. That's them. And special thanks to Sara for that day at Saratoga when I was scared and needed to ask for help and she didn't hesitate to be there for me. And she has continued to look out for me years later.

Ducky: You thanked Sara twice.

Me: Two different people. Same name.

Ducky: Humans are weird.

Me: On occasion.

Ducky: How about the internet people?

Me: Right. I started blogging on tumblr in August 2009 and the nature of the platform drove the creation of Ducky posts that form the basis for this book. And the creative community on tumblr consistently provided inspiration for "Well, That's Just Great," where the posts first appeared, and later on at your blog "Well, That's Just Ducky."

Ducky: ...

Me: ...

Ducky: I meant the internet people who like me.

Me: Of course! They've been amazing but there are far too many of them to mention by name.

Ducky: Lazy.

Me: On occasion. But in this case there truly were hundreds of people who not only read our posts, but reblogged them on their sites, and shared them on Facebook, and sent us notes encouraging us to turn the posts into a book. Without them there'd be no reason for the book and I'd certainly never have had the confidence to move forward with writing it.

Ducky: Lazy.

Me: ...

Ducky: Didn't people give us money for extra treats to keep my creative juices flowing?

Me: No. But people did contribute to our campaign on Indiegogo to help defray the costs of producing the book. Without them we might not have been able to afford to release the book when we did.

Ducky: ...

Me: ...

Ducky: I bet if you asked them they wouldn't mind you spending some of the money on extra treats to keep my creative juices flowing.

Me: Probably not. So maybe we'll get you a few extra after we're done with this.

Ducky: ...

Me: Don't worry. We're almost done. I need to thank my parents and my big brother and his family. They've been amazingly supportive of the project and of me. Especially over these past few difficult years.

Ducky: Don't forget The Lady.

Me: No. Don't worry. I can't forget her.

Ducky: She's nice.

Me: Yes. It's been a long strange trip for me and her. I'm glad she's by our side now. In addition to everything else she brings into our lives, she's been completely supportive of this project. Even when I haven't been.

Ducky: Love The Lady.

Me: Yeah. Me too. A lot. And her family.

Ducky: I'm glad we dedicated this to Foley. I miss her.

Me: Me too. She was a good sister to you.

Ducky: Even when she was trying to eat my face.

Me: Even then.

Ducky: Yeah.

Me: And thank you, Ducky.

Ducky: And thank you, Daddy. I love you.

Me: I love you too, Ducky.

Well That's Just Ducky! A Dog Is Man's Best Therapist

Anthony Giffen & Ducky

MOVING DAY

It made sense that I took Ducky.

Belle and I had two dogs. They'd gotten along fine, but we knew they wouldn't be traumatized by being separated from each other. At least, I believe that "we knew" that. As with most things during our life together, Belle and I found ourselves on the same page without needing to talk about it. So even though Belle would be keeping the house with the fenced-in yard, I would take the bigger dog to live with me in my second floor, one bedroom apartment of marital failure. Foley, the beagle we had adopted as a puppy thirteen years prior, would get to stay in the house with Belle, or as she was called when we talked to the dogs, "The Mama."

We were separating, not divorcing. Not yet. We had done all the things we believed we could do while still living together to fix what wasn't working and had reached a point where we realized we were neither miserable enough to feel that we had to divorce, nor were we in the kind of relationship that either of us could call fulfilling. We were best friends, and while we both believed that friendship was an important ingredient for a successful marriage, neither of us thought it was the only one. By separating we would either realize that we needed desperately to save our thirteen year marriage or that we were ready to move on with the next parts of our lives; parts neither of us had foreseen as even remote possibilities just six years earlier when we adopted Ducky.

At least, I believe that neither of us had foreseen those possibilities.

The first night alone was the fourth of July. I stood in the parking lot of my new apartment complex and saw fireworks exploding in the distance. Six years prior Belle and I had seen those fireworks from the window of our car as we drove to spend our first night in the home we had just bought.

I went back up to my apartment and realized that I hadn't unpacked Ducky's medications yet. He'd started having seizures a few years earlier but we'd found the right mix of pills to keep him healthy and episode free as long as we gave them to him on a consistent schedule. "Idiot." I mumbled at myself "One day. You can't even go one day without messing this up." I pressed the pills into some bread and popped them into Ducky's mouth before shuffling over to the futon sofa. It was the first piece of furniture Belle and I had ever bought together and one of the few things I had taken from home. I slumped down into it as Ducky walked up and placed his chin on my knee.

"Do you even know what's going on, Ducky? Do you know why we're here?"

Ducky looked up. His big, brown eyes and expressive brows always helped him appear to be quite thoughtful and made him often look as if he was trying to figure out what I was saying.

"..."

"I'm really scared, Duck," I admitted to the only one who could listen. He exhaled and looked away. I scratched him behind his ears.

"..."

I don't know if I can handle this. I'm not a strong man. I'm not mentally strong."

"..."

"I don't know what I'm doing. And I don't think I'm smart enough to figure it out alone.

"..."

Ducky jumped up on the futon, laid his head in my lap, and looked up at me.

"You're not alone, Daddy."

He stretched out and laid his head sideways. I scratched beneath his chin and he narrowed his eyes sleepily. It had been a long day for him too.

"No, Ducky. I guess I'm not."

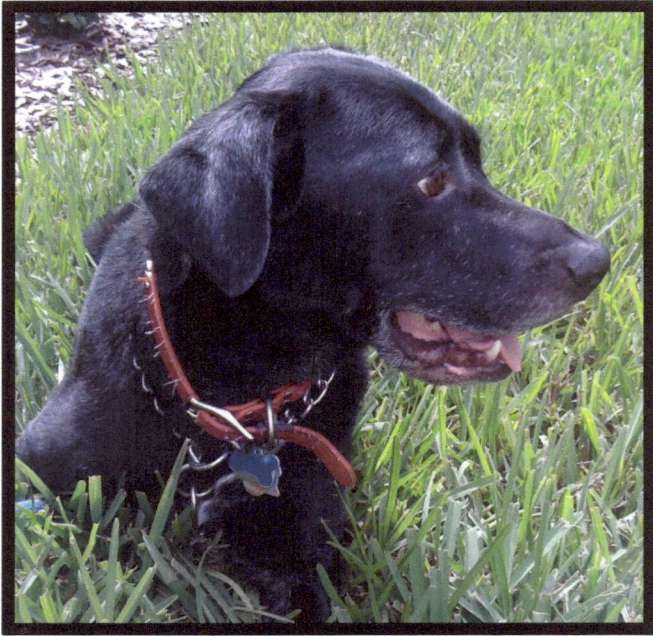

SIX MONTHS LATER

Ducky: Did you hear that?

Me: Yes, Ducky. Now poop.

Ducky: I think it was a mountain lion.

Me: It was not a mountain lion. Poop.

Ducky: Could have been a mountain lion.

Me: That seems unlikely in an apartment complex in Florida, a state with no mountains. Poop.

Ducky: …

Me: …

Ducky: Florida panther?

Me: No. Just another dog…uh oh.

Ducky: You said what now?

Me: No. It's another dog, but...

Ducky: ANOTHER DOGGIE?!?! WOO HOO!!! WHERE?! WHERE?!

Me: Way over there. Very, very far over there.

Ducky: Ooh! I see! Doesn't seem that far!

Me: It's further than it seems. Poop.

Ducky: The doggie is looking over here!

Me: Miles away. A lack of mountains can skew one's perception of distance. Poop.

Ducky: There's time for pooping later, man! There's a doggie over there!

Me: Yes, a doggie whose person is also trying to get her to poop. Perhaps before she has to go to work. Just like me.

Ducky: Two hers? Come on! It could be win-win!

Me: The Mama and I are still just separated, Ducky.

Ducky: Did she leave because you also kept *her* from pursuing her dreams?

Me: ...

Ducky: ...

Me: Only partially. And no one left anyone. We separated...

Ducky: Tell it to the head doctor. Let's go over for me then!

Me: You're been neutered anyway.

Ducky: …

Me: …

Ducky: We agreed to never…

Me: I know. I'm sorry.

Ducky: I'm just looking for a sniff anyway. Maybe her person will let you sniff her too …

Me: Unlikely.

Ducky: Don't knock it, old man.

Me: Poop.

Ducky: …

Me: …

Ducky: …

Me: Look, if you poop quickly enough maybe they'll still be there and if it looks like they're done, I promise we'll try to walk by them for a sniff. At least for you. I probably won't sniff the lady.

Ducky: Promise?

Me: Yes, even though I'm late for work, I promise.

Ducky: Thanks, Daddy.

Me: You're welcome.

Ducky: Oh, and Daddy?

Me: Yes, Ducky?

Ducky: If it is a Florida panther…

Me: I know. You will bark a lot and keep your distance and I will attack it.

Ducky: Teamwork! Thanks, Daddy! I love you.

Me: I love you too, Ducky. Now please poop.

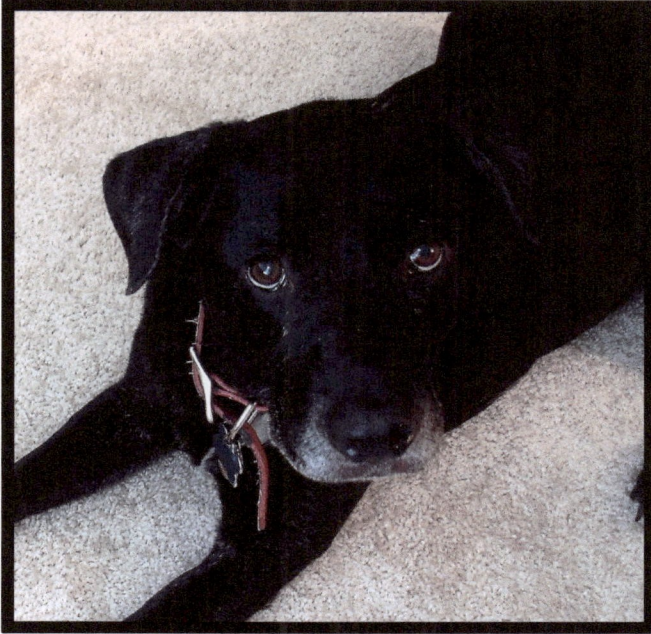

JANUARY

Ducky: Oops.

Me: No.

Ducky: Whoops?

Me: Stop it. Once is a whoops. Every day for a week is not an accident.

Ducky: No, every day would be plural. So they would be accident**S**!

Me: Don't play vocabulary games with me, dog. You are pooping on the carpet on purpose. You're frustrated and you're trying to hurt me.

Ducky: …

Me: …

Ducky: Uh-oh, SpaghettiOs®!?

Me: That's before your time.

Ducky: Not if you calculate it in dog years.

Me: That's not how that works.

Ducky: Maybe someone is pooping on the carpet because someone's daddy isn't coming home when he's supposed to and someone can't hold it any longer.

Me: That might be true for the days when someone's daddy is actually late. But *someone* has been doing it in the middle of the day, on weekends, even when it's the normal schedule. You're acting out.

Ducky: …

Me: …

Ducky: I tripped.

Me: That doesn't even make sense.

Ducky: Woof?

Me: Oh no! Don't act like you don't understand me!

Ducky: It's a desperate cry for attention. I wish you gave me positive feedback but I'll take your disappointment over your increasing emotional distance.

Me: ...

Ducky: Arf.

Me: I'm sorry about my schedule, but it should start getting better soon.

Ducky: Heard it all before. I mean, bow wow!

Me: Ugh. Listen, until you get this under control I'm going to keep you in the bathroom while I'm out. Smaller space. If that doesn't work, back to crate training.

Ducky: NOT THE BOX! NOT THE BOX!

Me: Oh, cut it out, you never minded the crate.

Ducky: That's when we still lived at the house with Foley and The Mama. The crate kept me safe.

Me: Safe from The Mama? You know the she could have opened the crate and gotten to you if she wanted, right?

Ducky: ...

Me: Thumbs are awesome.

Ducky: Ha, ha, ha. Hard to believe any woman would want to take a break from such wit.

Me: ...

Ducky: Sorry.

Me: ...

Ducky: You know I meant safe from the hellhound.

Me: Beagle. And half your size, you big baby.

Ducky: Submissive. It's a dog thing.

Me: Anyway, I'm sorry for my schedule but this has to improve. All we've got is each other. We don't need this extra stress.

Ducky: ...

Me: ...

Ducky: Okay. I'm sorry. I'll try.

Me: Thanks. I'll do my best to get home earlier whenever I can.

Ducky: Thank you.

Me: ...

Ducky: Dad?

Me: Yes?

Ducky: Did you ever poop on a carpet because you were lonely?

Me: No. No, I never have.

Ducky: Ever act out inappropriately and end up hurting others because you were lonely?

Me: ...

Ducky: ...

Me: Woof.

FEBRUARY

Ducky: You okay, Daddy?

Me: Yeah.

Ducky: ...

Me: Sorry about last night.

Ducky: You sounded pretty upset. Did something happen? Did you lose a toy? Did someone make you take a pill without peanut butter or bread?

Me: Ha. No. Just feeling lonely.

Ducky: Ah, I understand. That's how I feel when you go to work. But you always come back so I can deal.

Me: Yeah. It's a different kind of lonely, Duck. You wouldn't understand.

Ducky: …

Me: …

Ducky: I love you, Daddy.

Me: I love you too, Ducky.

Ducky: …

Me: …

Ducky: You know you weren't my first Daddy, right?

Me: Yeah. But I don't know anything about him really.

Ducky: …

Me: …

Ducky: I loved my first Daddy very much. He took care of me when I was very young. He taught me how to sit, and shake paws, and walk on a leash. He fed me. He gave me toys. He pet me. He made me feel very special.

Me: ...

Ducky: And then one day he left. And left me behind.

Me: ...

Ducky: ...

Me: At that apartment complex.

Ducky: Yup. And I looked for him for a long time. And when I couldn't find him I waited for him to come back. And when he didn't come back, I just sat in those fields and spent my days wondering what I did to drive him away. And if I was going to be alone forever.

Me: ...

Ducky: ...

Me: Sorry, Duck. That must have been awful.

Ducky: But then Judy showed up.

Me: From the shelter.

Ducky: I was kind of a mess. But she cleaned me up, and took care of me, gave me a place to live, and was a really good friend to me when I needed it. If she hadn't found me I don't know what would have happened.

Me: I'm glad she was there for you. She's a good person.

Ducky: Yeah. But not a daddy.

Me: ...

Ducky: Do you remember when you found me?

Me: At that event at work. Your Mama and I had lost Sam a few months earlier. We were still hurting from missing him. We had had Foley but didn't know if we were ready to adopt another dog.

Ducky: ...

Me: But we walked around the corner and there you were.

Ducky: Yup. With those two younger, cuter puppies in the crate right next to me.

Me: Yeah. I opened up your crate and you crawled right onto my lap. Like you belonged there.

Ducky: Uh huh. That's where I was supposed to be.

Me: ...

Ducky: And I didn't know it until it you were right there in front of me. Until then I really thought I would never have another Daddy. Not a real one.

Me: A real one?

Ducky: Dogs can tell when they have a real daddy and when they're just being "kept" because they're fun or cute.

Me: ...

Ducky: But you were real. And I found my home that day. I still love and miss my first Daddy. I probably always will. But I am so glad to be here with you.

Me: Yeah.

Ducky: Being lonely and scared hurt, but it got me to a place where I found my real Daddy. So taking the long view, I think it was worth the pain.

Me: …

Ducky: You're gonna' be okay, Daddy.

Me: ...

Ducky: ...

Me: Thanks, Duck. Love you.

Ducky: Love you too, Daddy.

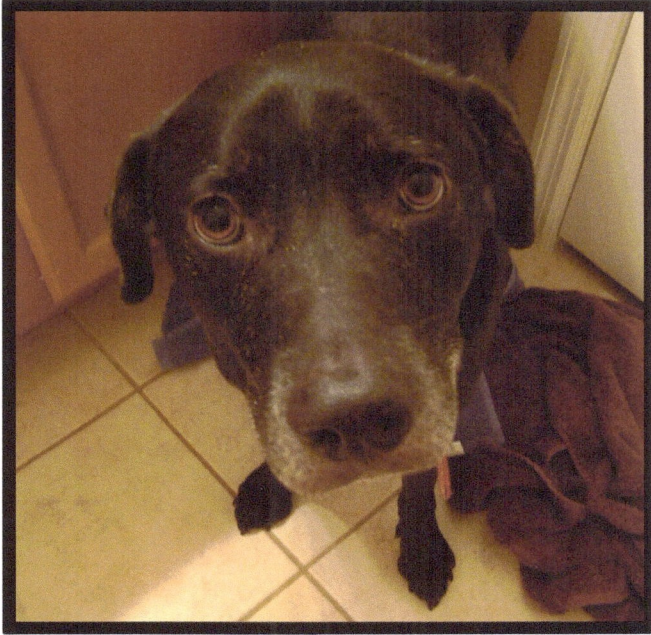

MARCH

Ducky: It wasn't my fault.

Me: I know.

Ducky: You know what you forgot to do?

Me: Close the door to your room before I left.

Ducky: EXACTLY.

Me: …

Ducky: So I stayed in there like 74 hours…

Me: I've been gone nine hours. But dogs have no sense of time, so go on.

Ducky: …

Me: …

Ducky: That's a myth.

Me: Sorry.

Ducky: Well, eventually I come out because I figured you must have left the door open for a reason. And I'm wandering around and I go in the bathroom. JUST to make sure you aren't in there….

Me: And the door closed behind you.

Ducky: And THE DOOR CLOSED BEHIND ME!

Me: And you couldn't get out.

Ducky: And I COULD NOT get out!

Me: No lights either, huh?

Ducky: NO! It was daaaaaaarrrrk!

Me: I would imagine. So you…?

Ducky: Started occupying myself.

Me: By?

Ducky: ...

Me: Eating my clothes.

Ducky: Eating your clothes, yes.

Me: So exactly how much...

Ducky: Two socks consumed in total, one brown and one black. One pair of underwear half eaten.

Me: I thought dogs were colorblind?

Ducky: ...

Me: ...

Ducky: That's a myth.

Me: Ah!

Ducky: But shirts, shorts, and towels left completely untouched!

Me: ...

Ducky: ...

Me: Then what are you currently sitting...

Ducky: Left completely unchewed!

Me: Thank you for that.

Ducky: …

Me: …

Ducky: Sorry I got scared.

Me: It's okay. Sorry I forgot to close the doors.

Ducky: Love you, Daddy. Glad you're home.

Me: I love you too, Ducky.

Ducky: …

Me: …

Ducky: Daddy?

Me: Yes, Ducky?

Ducky: I should probably explain why the soap is missing.

.

APRIL

Me: We gonna talk about it, Ducky?

Ducky: Talk about what? Everything's fine.

Me: ...

Ducky: ...

Me: Ducky, I'm sorry I left.

Ducky: You were gone for a long time.

Me: I thought dogs had no real sense of time?

Ducky: That's a myth. We know when people are gone longer than usual. You were gone a lot longer than usual.

Me: I know. But you got to go back to the house and stay with The Mama. And Foley.

Ducky: Love the Mama. Hate Cerberus.

Me: Aw, that's not true. Foley was so sad to see you go when I picked you up.

Ducky: The hellhound is a liar. You don't know what she's like when you leave. Or even when you just turn your back. Stupid alpha dogs.

Me: You love Foley.

Ducky: ...

Me: You had a yard again for awhile.

Ducky: The yard reeked of beagle.

Me: I'm sorry, Ducky. I really needed the time away.

Ducky: From me?

Me: Oh, stop that. You know I love you. You also know how stressed I've been.

Ducky: Yeah. You were even making me tense. You should try yoga.

Me: Maybe.

Ducky: Mindfulness meditation.

Me: ...

Ducky: Namaste.

Me: I'll consider those in the future, Lama. But the opportunity for a trip came up and it felt like the right choice.

Ducky: ...

Me: ...

Ducky: Where'd you go?

Me: Disneyland.

Ducky: ...

Me: ...

Ducky: You go there a lot.

Me: No, I go to Disney World. That's the one here in Florida.

Ducky: ...

Me: Disneyland is in California.

Ducky: Sounds similar.

Me: They are similar.

Ducky: What makes the one you went to different?

Me: Um, it's older.

Ducky: ...

Me: Smaller.

Ducky: ...

Me: For us, a lot farther away.

Ducky: ...

Me: I needed to pay to stay in a hotel to go to that one.

Ducky: Sounds great.

Me: Now that you mention it...

Ducky: So why go there.?

Me: I was able to go with some friends.

Ducky: Friends from California?

Me: ...

Ducky: ...

Me: No. They live here too.

Ducky: ...

Me: We ran a half marathon out there.

Ducky: Uh huh. Don't you run those here?

Me: Yeah.

Ducky: ...

Me: ...

Ducky: Humans are weird.

Me: Now that you mention it.

Ducky: But if it made you happy, I guess it was a good idea.

Me: Yeah. It was good to get away. It really didn't matter where. They were going, they invited me, and it was nice to just have fun again.

Ducky: You look more relaxed.

Me: I am.

Ducky: Did you have an epiphany out there? Moment of clarity? Develop a new way to process stressful stimuli?

Me: No. Had an awesome corn dog though.

Ducky: Food?

Me: Oh yeah. Lots of food.

Ducky: Now I understand. Glad it helped, Daddy.

Me: Thanks, Duck.

Ducky: Yeah. But you don't do that again, ok?

Me: Ok, Ducky. At least not for awhile.

Ducky: ...

Me: ...

Ducky: So…what did you bring me?

Me: Maybe I won a little stuffed duckie that I'm saving for you for a special day.

Ducky: Mondays are special.

Me: Let's go back inside, Ducky. You're due a few belly rubbings.

Ducky: Glad you're home, Daddy.

Me: Me too, Duck.

Ducky: I love you, Daddy.

Me: I love you, Ducky.

MAY

Me: Why you smilin', Ducky?

Ducky: I'm happy, Daddy.

Me: Why are you happy, Ducky?

Ducky: Just am.

Me: Sounds nice.

Ducky: ...

Me: ...

Ducky: You unhappy, Daddy?

Me: Generally, yes.

Ducky: ...

Me: ...

Ducky: You can be happy too, Daddy.

Me: I know.

Ducky: Why aren't you happy, Daddy?

Me: A combination of genetics, societal factors, work stressors, ineffective coping strategies, increased resistance to drugs, and a lack of direction in life.

Ducky: …

Me: Just am.

Ducky: Sorry.

Me: ...

Ducky: It's okay to be unhappy. But you should let yourself be happy when you want to be.

Me: Working on it, Ducky.

Ducky: Okay. I love you. Happy or not.

Me: Thanks, Duck.

Ducky: ...

Me: ...

Ducky: Wanna go eat? That makes us both happy.

Me: Sounds good, Duck.

Ducky: Love you, Daddy.

Me: Love you, Ducky.

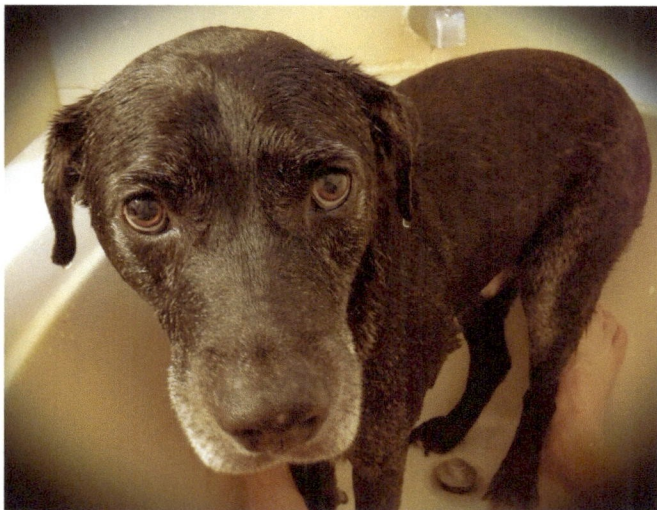

JUNE

Ducky: This is weird.

Me: I thought it might make bath time less stressful.

Ducky: I didn't know baths made you stressed.

Me: Not me, you.

Ducky: I don't like baths.

Me: I am aware of that.

Ducky: And you thought adding another body to the tub would make it more enjoyable?

Me: It's like a party.

Ducky: …

Me: Party in the tub!

Ducky: This is weird.

Me: Well sue me for trying something new.

Ducky: You're wearing pants in the bath tub. That's weird.

Me: It's a swimsuit.

Ducky: I'm not wearing a swimsuit. Why are you?

Me: If I wasn't this would be weird.

Ducky: …

Me: Weirder.

Ducky: Rinse me, old man.

Me: Me first.

Ducky: Weirdo.

Me: I love you, Ducky.

Ducky: I love you, Daddy.

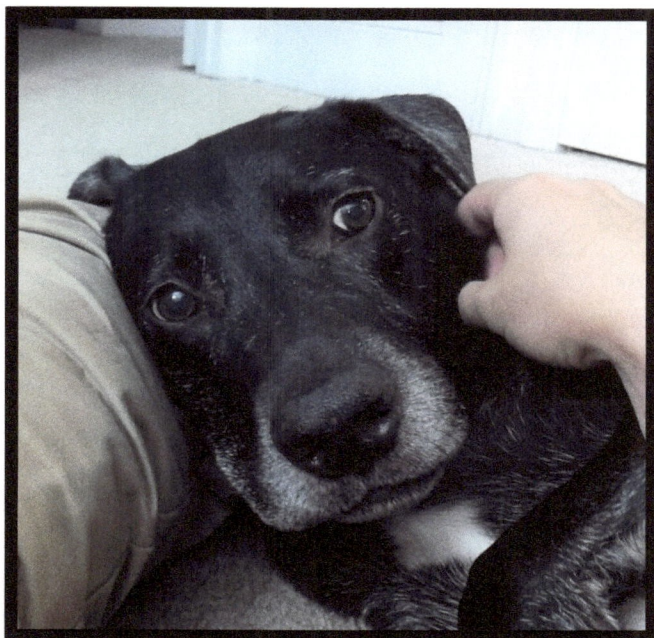

JULY

Ducky: Hey, Daddy?

Me: Yes, Ducky?

Ducky: What happens when you die?

Me: Wow. I don't know, Ducky. No one knows.

Ducky: ...

Me: I've always thought dogs like you go to a special place where you get to run free all the time, and not have seizures, and eat when you want and as much as you want.

Ducky: That sounds nice.

Me: Yeah. I think dogs earn that place. And I think it's the kind of place where, if you wanted, you would be able to leave to check in on me sometimes.

Ducky: Yeah? Like see you?

Me: Yeah. I think you're gonna meet Sniffles and Sam and you're going to get along really well because you were all my dogs.

Ducky: You think?

Me: Yup. I still think I see Sniffles and Sam out of the corner of my eye sometimes. So I think they're around when they want to be; when I need them. But for the most part I think they run around and have fun because they know that I have you looking out for me. So I think that's what will happen if you go. You'll be having a great time but sometimes you'll come back and be beside me. I won't see you but I'll feel you. And I'll remember you.

Ducky: ...

Me: ...

Ducky: Sounds okay.

Me: ...

Ducky: But what happens if you die? Where do you go?

Me: That I don't know.

Ducky: ...

Me: ...

Ducky: But you think you know where dogs go?

Me: Yeah.

Ducky: ...

Me: I know that's weird.

Ducky: A little.

Me: But I'm not going to die for a long time.

Ducky: Promise?

Me: Promise.

Ducky: ...

Me: ...

Ducky: Promise?

Me: I promise, Ducky. We've gotten past the worst. I'm not giving up on this ride yet. Besides. I want as much time with you as I can possibly get. I'm greedy for Ducky time!

Ducky: ...

Me: I'm not going anywhere.

Ducky: Okay, but what about an accident? You could get hit by a car or get heartworms.

Me: Well, if I died by accident I'm sure The Mama would take you back right away.

Ducky: Promise?

Me: I promise. She loves you very much and would never let you be alone.

Ducky: …

Me: …

Ducky: If you go to a place like the one you talked about, and I go live with the Mama, when you weren't running and playing with other people would you check in on me sometime?

Me: Absolutely. Whenever you needed me and sometimes just because…

Ducky: Okay. Thanks, Daddy.

Me: You're welcome, Duck.

Ducky: ...

Me: ...

Ducky: Don't die.

Me: You too.

Ducky: Ok

Me: Love you, Ducky.

Ducky: Love you too, Dad.

AUGUST

Ducky: …

Me: …

Ducky: You lied.

Me: Ducky…

Ducky: You said, "Just the blood test. And then home."

Me: That's...

Ducky: "Just making sure your seizure medication is at the right level.'"

Me: I know. But your nails needed a trim and you won't let me do it…

Ducky: And WHY don't I let you do it?

Me: Because I cut the quick once. And you bled a little.

Ducky: A LITTLE? It looked like a Tarantino film was shot in the kitchen!

Me: …

Ducky: If you know it, I know it, film buff!

Me: Makes sense.

Ducky: So you take me to the trusted professionals and even though it's just a blood test day, you say, "Clip the nails while you're here!"

Me: I know.

Ducky: And what happens?

Me: They cut the quick.

Ducky: THEY CUT THE QUICK! And then what do they do to make things better?

Me: It wasn't to make things better, Ducky…

Ducky: They clean out my ears. You know what I hate, Daddy?

Me: Having your ears cleaned.

Ducky: HAVING MY EARS CLEANED!!!

Me: Look, I know, but when they find stuff…

Ducky: Glad I bled all over their office. Made it look like a Peckinpah film in there.

Me: …

Ducky: …

Me: I'm sorry, Ducky.

Ducky: Yeah, Yeah, Yeah.

Me: …

Ducky: …

Me: …

Ducky: Dad. My paws and ears hurt.

Me: I'm sorry, Ducky. We'll be home soon and I'll give you some treats and we'll both rest.

Ducky: Sorry I'm grumpy.

Me: I know. I don't blame you.

Ducky: ...

Me: ...

Ducky: Should I be worried about the blood tests?

Me: I don't think so. It's just a check to make sure your medications are at exactly the right level. They always are. This is just being extra careful.

Ducky: Okay.

Me: Besides, worrying doesn't do any good.

Ducky: Doesn't stop you.

Me: I know. I guess you picked that up from me too.

Ducky: So are you worried about the blood tests?

Me: I always worry about your blood tests, Ducky.

Ducky: Sorry.

Me: It's okay. I just love ya, Duck. Want you to be healthy for a long, long time. Need you around.

Ducky: I love you too, Daddy.

Me: …

Ducky: …

Me: You're bleeding on that seat aren't you?

Ducky: …

Me: …

Ducky: Maybe.

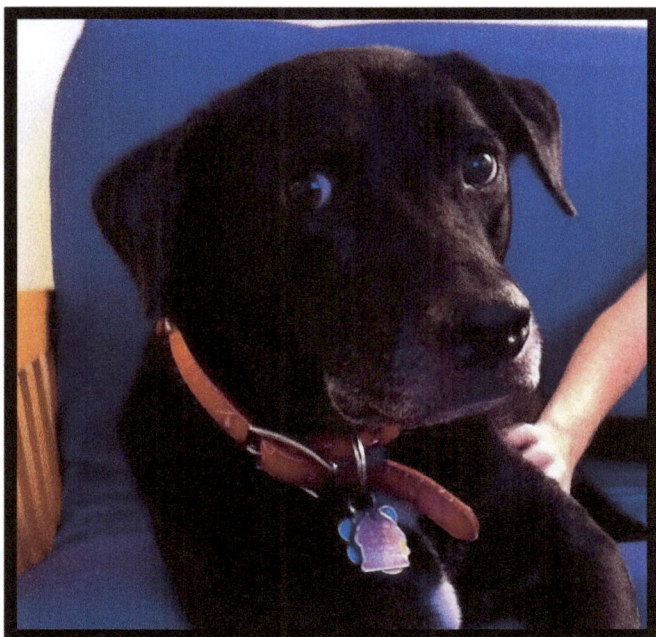

SEPTEMBER

Friend: That's so neat.

Me: What?

Friend: How obedient Ducky is.

Ducky: Pardon?

Me: You hear that Ducky? She thinks you've very obedient.

Ducky: I prefer the word cooperative.

Friend: …

Me: As the guy who deals with you the most I'd say neither word is totally appropriate.

Friend: Oh my God.

Ducky & Me: What?

Friend: You really do have conversations with your dog.

Me: …

Ducky: …

Me: …

Ducky: Woof.

OCTOBER

Ducky: Daddy?

Me: Yeah, Duck?

Ducky: You, okay?

Me: Meh. A little down. No big deal.

Ducky: Why?

Me: Oh. I've just had a lot of reminders lately of mistakes I've made, opportunities I've let slip by, bad things I've done….

Ducky: Like pooping in the house?

Me: Not literally, no, but the human equivalent.

Ducky: …

Me: The Mama and I are finalizing the divorce.

Ducky: Oh.

Me: And I'm not doing a great job at work. I used to be really good at my job, but with moving and separating I've really let things slide.

Ducky: Oh. And that makes you sad?

Me: Right now it does. Right now it makes me feel like I don't deserve happiness. If I'm a failed husband, and a failing professional, what right do I have to be happy?

Ducky: …

Me: …

Ducky: You don't play with me enough, Daddy.

Me: …

Ducky: And sometimes you stay out too late and leave me alone a long time.

Me: Really, Duck?

Ducky: And you don't pet me anywhere near as much as you used to. When your friends come over they pay much more attention to me than you do.

Me: ...

Ducky: ...

Me: Are dogs familiar with the concept of "jumping on the pile," Ducky?

Ducky: Oh, and I hate those baths.

Me: Do you have a point, dog?

Ducky: I love you, Daddy.

Me: …

Ducky: You're not perfect, but you're not supposed to be. You're just supposed to be my Daddy. And you're great at that.

Me: …

Ducky: And I've seen other people who seem to like you and love you even though you think you're not so great all the time. The Mama still loves you. And those new people who pet me all the time seem to like you just the way you are.

Me: …

Ducky: Am I perfect, Daddy?

Me: Far from it.

Ducky: Does it make you love me less?

Me: …no. Not at all.

Ducky: And those things that you did don't make your friends or me love you any less.

Me: …

Ducky: …

Me: No?

Ducky: Nope. And mistakes don't make you deserve unhappiness.

Me: …

Ducky: Have you tried to correct your mistakes?

Me: As best as I can.

Ducky: Have you learned from them and are you going to try to not make those mistakes again?

Me: Yes.

Ducky: Well then I think punishing yourself forever by not allowing happiness back into your life is stupid.

Me: Yeah?

Ducky: Yes. And I'm a dog so I'm seven times smarter than a human so you should listen to me.

Me: I don't think that's how it works. I think that's just with age.

Ducky: That's a myth. But I forgive you and love you, Daddy.

Me: I love you, Ducky.

Ducky: But a little more petting wouldn't hurt.

Me: Fair enough.

NOVEMBER

Me: Hey, Duck. What are you doing there?

Ducky: Just gettin' ready for bed. Can you get the light?

Me: You don't sleep on the futon, Ducky, I do.

Ducky: I know. But that bed in the other room just goes unused. You could sleep there. And I could sleep here.

Me: …

Ducky: Dogs sleep on futons. Daddies sleep in beds.

Me: Actually dogs sleep on the floor.

Ducky: You're missing the bigger point.

Me: …

Ducky: It's just a bed.

Me: It's the guest bed from the house.

Ducky: It was. Now it's just a bed.

Me: …

Ducky: I know it makes you think about what you lost.

Me: …

Ducky: The divorce was finalized today, right?

Me: Yeah.

Ducky: …

Me: …

Ducky: What did you say to your friend about this being the start of the third chapter of your life?

Me: You heard that, huh?

Ducky: Chapter One: Young Daddy. Chapter Two: Married Daddy. And now..

Me: Daddy of Unknown Future.

Ducky: A bit dramatic but an okay working title for the third chapter.

Me: ...

Ducky: Maybe that chapter can start with not assigning unnecessarily great emotional value to things that fundamentally have none.

Me: Pardon?

Ducky: Sleep in the bed enough and it'll become just a bed. Not a symbol.

Me: …

Ducky: I mean, "Woof!"

Me: Do you just want to sleep on the futon?

Ducky: It plays a role.

Me: ...

Ducky: ...

Me: Okay. We'll try it.

Ducky: I think that's a good idea, Daddy.

Me: Me too. Thanks, Ducky. Love you.

Ducky: I love you, Daddy. Good night.

DECEMBER

Ducky: Going to the vet?

Me: Yeah.

Ducky: Oh.

Me: What?

Ducky: I thought maybe we were going to the dog park.

Me: No. Ducky. I'm sorry. The vet needs to test you to make sure your meds are still helping you.

Ducky: So maybe we go to the dog park after?

Me: Sorry, Duck.

Ducky: Got plans? Got to hurry me back home?

Me: …

Ducky: …

Me: I'm sorry I don't take you to the dog park anymore, Ducky.

Ducky: …

Me: …

Ducky: Did I do something wrong?

Me: No. Nothing at all. It's just that last time we went there was a guy who didn't like you because he thought you were a certain type of dog.

Ducky: …

Me: …

Ducky: He thought I was a beagle?

Me: No.

Ducky: ...

Me: He thought you looked like a mean dog.

Ducky: ...

Me: ...

Ducky: Did I do something mean to him?

Me: No. You never do. You were doing your usual thing...

Ducky: Running up to other dogs and trying to get them to beat me up?

Me: That's right, my submissive friend. You kept nudging other dogs and then you rolling on your back like you always do.

Ducky: Why did that make him think I was a mean dog?

Me: It didn't. He decided you were a mean dog the second he saw you. Some people think they can tell that by appearance.

Ducky: ...

Me: ...

Ducky: That's stupid.

Me: Yeah.

Ducky: But why would that stop you from taking me there?

Me: He said if he ever saw you there he would call animal control at the first sign of "trouble."

Ducky: Trouble?

Me: Yeah.

Ducky: Like running up to another dog?

Me: Maybe. He seemed to consider that troublesome behavior at a dog park.

Ducky: ...

Me: ...

Ducky: But then you and the other nice people could explain to animal control that I'm not mean.

Me: Unfortunately, they might not believe us. They might just decide to take you away from me. It happens. Some people lose their dogs for not very good reasons.

Ducky: Oh.

Me: And I'm sorry, Duck, I can't risk losing you.

Ducky: Yeah. I understand. But that sucks. The jerk wins.

Me: Jerks win sometimes, Ducky. But part of being an adult means not letting your pride cost you what really matters.

Ducky: I matter?

Me: You matter a lot. So I let it go. And I focus on the good. I like playing at home with you.

Ducky: I like that too.

Me: So, I'm sorry that we don't go to the dog park anymore.

Ducky: It's okay. I'll let it go! And focus on what really matters. I love you, Daddy.

Me: I love you too, Ducky.

Ducky: …

Me: …

Ducky: But what a jerk.

Me: Yeah.

NEW YEAR'S EVE

Ducky: It's a fuzzy duck.

Me: Yup.

Ducky: Like me.

Me: Sorta'.

Ducky: It's soft and fluffy and delicate.

Me: Yup.

Ducky: I'm going to destroy it in about three minutes.

Me: I think three minutes is generous. I'm surprised it's not gone already.

Ducky: And that's okay?

Me: Does it make you happy?

Ducky: Yup.

Me: Then it's ok.

Ducky: Thanks.

Me: I won it for you in Disneyland.

Ducky: You were there a long time ago.

Me: About eight months ago.

Ducky: And you were having fun with human friends.

Me: Yup.

Ducky: And you thought to get something for me?

Me: Of course. You're my best buddy.

Ducky: Thanks, Daddy.

Me: ...

Ducky: ...

Me: It was a really bad year, Ducky.

Ducky: I know, Daddy.

Me: But in the middle of that bad year I had one of the happiest times of my life.

Ducky: You were happy when you were there.

Me: And during the worst year of my life, you were always there for me.

Ducky: You're my Daddy. It's what I do.

Me: So I wanted something to connect the two as we head into next year, you and me.

Ducky: Sounds nice. Shows that even in the bad times, things can make us happy if we let them.

Me: That's what you do, Ducky. Thanks. For everything.

Ducky: ...

Me: ...

Ducky: I can still continue destroying it, can't I?

Me: Of course. We are who we are.

Ducky: Thanks, Daddy. Happy New Year.

Me: Happy New Year.

Ducky: I love you, Daddy.

Me: I love you too, Ducky.

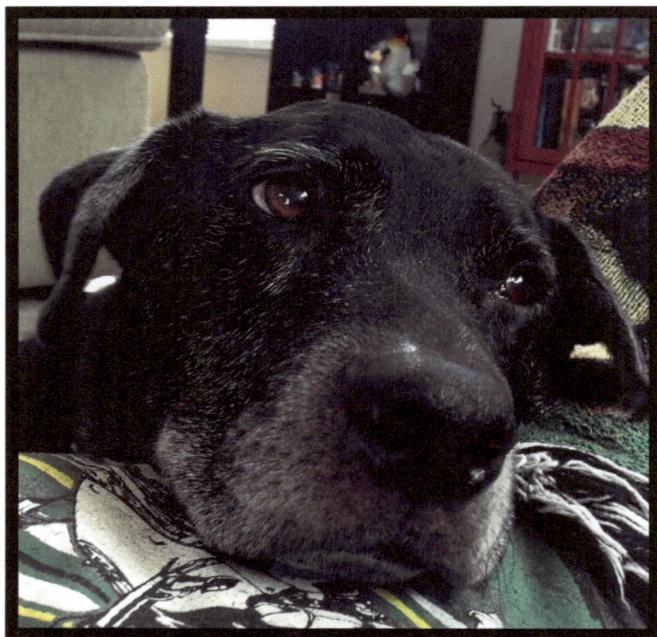

MOVING DAY

"So we're definitely not going back to the apartment?"

"No, Ducky. We're back in the house to stay."

Almost a year had passed since the divorce had been finalized. I was lying on the floor and Ducky was on his side with his back pressed up against me to demonstrate his support and affection; also so I could rub his belly and chest. Probably more because of that rubbing thing. Years of experience meant Ducky could tell that I was lying on the floor because I was tired from moving boxes, not because of any existential crisis.

"Explain to me again why we're back here."

When asked by friends and family, I had struggled to explain why Belle and I had decided that it made sense for me to take back the house. "It's between Belle and me," was sufficient to end most conversations when asked about why we divorced, but for some reason that response felt unnecessarily evasive when people were curious about why Ducky and I were moving back in. And if I was too opaque I worried that people would get the wrong idea and think Belle and I were attempting a reconciliation.

"There are lots of reasons, Ducky. But basically, The Mama was planning to move out and selling the house was going to be hard."

"Because of the problems in the real estate market fueled by the sub prime mortgage crisis?"

I made a mental note that perhaps I was leaving the television tuned to news channels too often and should consider Animal Planet as background noise in the future. "Yes, that played a role," I admitted. "So she asked if we would be interested in taking the house back. And I thought it was a good idea."

Ducky then asked what I felt confident that many of my friends and family members had been wondering, "You thought moving back into the house where your thirteen year marriage fell apart was a good idea?"

"I considered that factor and others and decided it was worth trying."

Ducky seemed to be contemplating whether or not to challenge me on that so I decided to appeal to his self-interest.

"Isn't it going to be nice," I asked, "to have a yard again?"

"Isn't is going to be nice, " he retorted, "to not have to take me out to go potty? Isn't it going to be nice to just roll out of bed and open the door and then crawl back into bed to sleep?"

"Yes it is," I admitted.

"Laziness trumps risk of possible emotional devastation."

"It can certainly hold its own."

"You're a lazy, lazy man, Daddy."

"I don't think there's going to be much emotional devastation, Ducky. Yes, this house was where the Mama and I first started having trouble. But it's also where we had a lot of good times. And it's where you first lived with us. And I'm choosing to focus on those memories as much as possible."

"Sounds healthy."

"And most importantly I'm going to make lots of new memories here with you!"

"And The Lady?"

I had started dating a friend soon after the divorce. She'd been spending a lot of time at the apartment. Ducky apparently had noticed.

"Yeah. I think The Lady's going to help us make some good memories too." I felt myself starting to nod off. Emotionally *devastating* or not, it had certainly been an emotional day. If that past New Year's Eve had marked the end of the life I had lived up until that point, this moment very much felt like the beginning of my new life; a life informed by my past but not dictated by it; a life that was moving forward, but towards what I could not say for certain. But after what I had been through the past few years, and what I had learned, I knew I could handle it.

I learned I was stronger than I thought I was. I learned that I wasn't alone. And I learned what really mattered to me; what was real; and what I needed to hold on to when things got difficult.

I gave Ducky a squeeze.

"I love you, Ducky."

"I love you, Daddy."

ABOUT THE AUTHORS

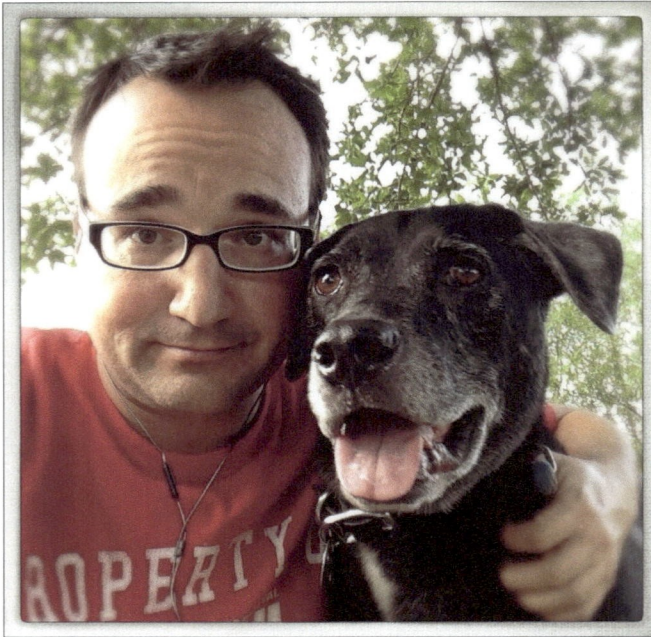

Anthony Giffen graduated from Millersville University in
Lancaster, Pennsylvania in 1995 with a BS in Education. After
graduation he made his living as an improvisational actor and
comedian for a few years before relocating to Central Florida in
1998. He's spent the last 15 years finding ways to leverage his
educational and improvisational experience in various operations,
training, human resource, consultation, and leadership positions. In
2009 he created "Well That's Just Great" on the tumblr platform as
a creative outlet for self expression. Since then he has also created
a partner site focused on leadership and, of course, the ongoing
home of the Ducky conversations, "Well, That's Just Ducky!"

Ducky Giffen is a dog. He is cute and would like you to pet him
and scratch him and feed him. He would like to re-emphasize the
feeding part. Providing him fuzzy things to destroy is also
appreciated. That is all.

FOLLOW THE DUCKY DOG!

Our Base For All Things "Well, Thats...!"
wellthats.com

Where It All Started!
wellthatsjustgreat.tumblr.com

Where It Lives!
wellthatsjustducky.tumblr.com

Anthony Giffen's Leadership Tumblr!
anthonygiffen.tumblr.com

www.ingramcontent.com/pod-product-compliance
Lightning Source LLC
Chambersburg PA
CBHW041522090426

42737CB00037B/8